Great TANK BATTLES of WW II

A Combat Diary of the Second World War

by GEORGE BRADFORD

maps by LORNE WILLIAMS

An AEROFACT Book
Published by ARCO PUBLISHING COMPANY, INC.

Second Printing, 1976

Published by Arco Publishing Company, Inc.
219 Park Avenue South, New York, N.Y. 10003

Copyright © 1970 by AEROFACT INC.

Library of Congress Catalog Card Number 77-106482
ISBN 0-668-02288-4

Printed in the United States of America

Introduction

The Second World War was truly the proving ground of the massive armored formations. In the years preceding the war, most countries agreed that armor was here to stay as an excellent support wing for the infantry divisions. However, there were only a few military men who could see far enough ahead to realize that this mobile force was eventually to rule the battlefield. Of these, German General Heinz Guderian alone managed to impress upon his superiors the great potential striking power of a purely armored formation.

Both De Gaulle of France and Elles of England had struggled for years to have this concept accepted by their military staffs, but both had gone unheeded. Time and unparalleled defeats were to bring the point home to all nations.

With this book we hope to trace the evolution and use of armor throughout World War II, and to highlight the more important battles in which armored forces played a part. Although the book title suggests tanks only, we will be touching on all armored vehicles, tracked or otherwise, which fall into the broad scope of the term "armor." The photographs provide a glimpse of the important armored vehicles in the war from all sides, but are by no means a total coverage. Priority has been given to those events that involved a large proportion of armored formations, but mention will be made of many other important battles which make up this period of history.

In order to maintain the proper chronology throughout, it has been necessary to continually depart from one theater of action to cover another. In this way, one is made aware of the whole structure of actions having a bearing on the manpower and supply problems of all sides involved.

Invasion of Poland

Left, when hostilities opened in 1939
Germany was equipped mainly with
Panzerkampfwagen I light tanks. The
formation left, is made up of the
early PzKpfw. I/A model (Odell).
Above, infantry supported by a PzKpfw. II
displaying the bold white cross that was
prominent in the Polish campaign

PzKpfw II(A,B) 20mm

In early dawn of September 1, 1939, Poland was attacked by Germany. At this point, Germany's panzer divisions were equipped mainly with the PzKpfw. I and II, plus the PzKpfw. 35t and 38t acquired through the conquest of Czechoslovakia. Of the 3,195 tanks in their mobile force, only 98 were PzKpfw. III's and 211 were PzKpfw. IV's with their short barrelled 75-mm guns. At least two-thirds of this force was directed against approximately 750 Polish vehicles made up of Vickers Six Tonners, 7TP, TK and TKS tankettes, R-35's, and some outdated armored cars. The German surprise onslaught moved far too fast for the Polish forces to counter, and they were soon divided by the northern and southern thrusts. The precise air-to-ground strikes made by the Luftwaffe cleared all resistance for the advancing armor.

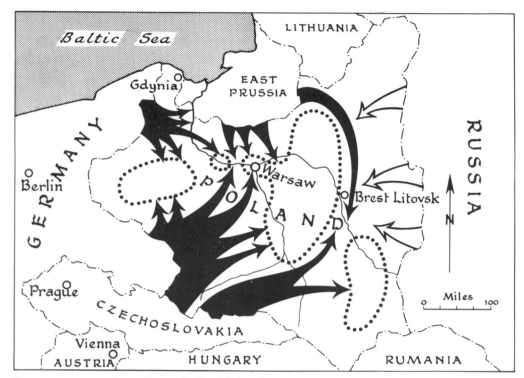

German armored formations slashed Poland in two, while the Russian entry from the east precluded any Polish regrouping.

A German PzSpw. SdKfz. 222 armored scout car used in reconnaissance roles *(Odell)*

PzSpw(Sd.Kfz 222) 20mm

A Polish TKS Tankett. *(Odell)*

With the Polish Air Force practically wiped out on the ground within the first two days, the Luftwaffe was free to attack communications. Actually, the Poles did not even manage to complete full mobilization of their armored forces, and their newly equipped battalion of French R-35 tanks never joined the action. Thus the German *Blitzkrieg* was given its baptism of fire and overwhelmed stubborn Polish resistance in less than three weeks. The fate of Poland was sealed even before Russia sent her forces into eastern Poland on September 17.

THE PHONY WAR: During this period French and Germans sat facing each other across their borders. France did make a probe into the Saar, and late in September the Germans drove them back to the Maginot Line. Germany spent the time strengthening her sadly inadequate Siegfried Line, and Britain and France concentrated on production of strategic war materials.

French R-35 tanks guarding the border during the period of the "Phony War" *(IWM)*

Russo-Finnish Conflict

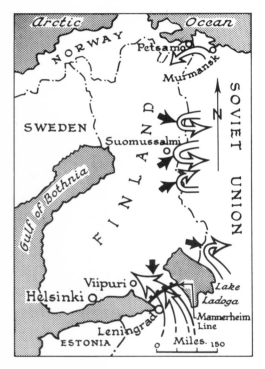

The Finnish defenses held all Russian attacks except at Petsam in the north. Mannerheim Line in south held initially, but fell to a larger attack in 1940.

Even though a peace treaty had been signed between Russia and Germany, Stalin was still wary of Hitler's intentions, and decided to bargain with Finland in order to strengthen Russia's western borders. He felt that Leningrad was far too vulnerable and tried to induce the Finns to move their border west on the Karelian Isthmus. When they refused, Russia bombed Helsinki and, on November 30th, deployed an army of nearly 500,000 men against Finland's borders. However, the Finns made skillful use of their winter terrain and in one sector alone, Suomussalmi, they annihilated two Russian divisions of about 30,000 men. The extreme winter conditions thwarted any decisive action by the superior Russian armored forces until February 1940, when they managed to hammer a hole in the Mannerheim Line and Finland surrendered to the Russian territorial demands.

A Russian BT7, prominent at the time of the Russo-Finish war

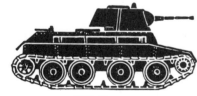

BT7 45mm

Germany Attacks in the West

German PzKpfw. I/B, part of
Reinforced Korps XXXI which entered
Denmark in 1940 *(Axel Duckert)*

PzKpfw I(B) MG

DENMARK OCCUPIED: On April 9, 1940, Hitler brought the passive winter months to a close by occupying Denmark, thereby guaranteeing German control of the Baltic Sea entrance.

SEIZURE OF NORWAY: With Denmark as a jumping-off base, Hitler reached out for Norway's iron mines, industry, and sea coast bases that were to prove so important in breaking the British blockade. Although British troops supported the Norwegians, and several German troop shipments were sunk, the overthrow of Norway went smoothly, and by the end of May Norway was completely in Hitler's hands.

Blitzkrieg in the West

French R-35 tanks moving into position *(IWM)*

Renault R35 37mm

With the Battle of France the full importance of the armored divisions was established. Although everyone knew of the events in Poland, it was assumed that the inferiority of Polish equipment had allowed the Germans to achieve a conclusive victory. However, the world was soon to learn otherwise. Although French armor on the whole was easily equal to the quality of the German tanks, it was employed in a completely different manner. The greater part of the French armor was spread throughout eight armies which stretched from the Swiss border to the English Channel. Germany, on the other hand, had adopted Guderian's theories and concentrated all her strength in ten Panzer divisions. Nine of these were massed on a narrow front of less than one hundred miles. Since they were concentrated into Panzer corps, they could launch a powerful breakthrough on the French front and exploit this by a quick thrust toward the channel coast. By now the Germans had built up the number of medium tanks in hand to 329 PzKpfw. III and 280 PzKpfw. IV, for a total of 3,379 tanks of all kinds. Against France they launched 2,570 tanks and some 600 armored cars. France met this with 2,500 modern tanks, mostly R-35 models, and 700 armored cars. The balance was made up of H-35, H-39, S-35, F. C. M., B-1, and even 2C and F. T. tanks of World War I vintage. The British had very little armor in the B. E. F., except for some Vickers Mk. VI light tanks, Mk. I and Mk. II Infantry tanks in small numbers. On the tenth of May the Germans launched their offensive in the west, and the routes through the forested heights of the Ardennes came alive with German tanks moving ahead, nose to tail. At the same time, the main pressure was applied against Holland and Belgium in order to draw the British and French forces into the Low Countries. By the evening of May 12 the Panzer divisions had reached the French border and by the thirteenth, Guderian's XIX Panzer Corps had stormed the Meuse at Sedan and Rommel's 7th Panzer Division had crossed at Dinant.

Knocked out French Char B-1 heavy tanks (*Warpics*)

British Evacuate Dunkirk

British Infantry Tank Mark I *(Odell)*

Now the Germans were in the open with nothing to oppose them except belated thrusts by small units. A spearhead of five armored divisions followed by two others cut a swath sixty miles wide between the Allied armies in France and Belgium. Advancing at a rate of thirty to forty miles a day, they reached the coast at Abbeville by May 21, and started to swing north to encircle the B. E. F. and French 1st and 7th Armies in the Flanders pocket. The British put up stiff resistance to permit withdrawal of troops at Dunkirk, but all their heavy equipment had to be abandoned.

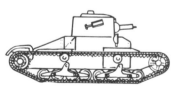

A11 Mk.I"Infantry" MG

Germans Take Paris

No sooner had the battle of Flanders ended than the Wehrmacht swiftly regrouped and re-deployed. On June 5, before the hastily formed Weygand Line could be effectively defended, the German forces struck south into France. With the Luftwaffe ruling the skies and the cream of the French Army lost at Flanders, the Germans had little trouble breaching the line. With a vast predominance in tanks, mechanized divisions and artillery, they put the French forces into headlong retreat. Paris was declared an open city and by June 14 was in German hands. By the sixteenth it was all but over and on June 21 the surrender ceremonies took place at Compiègne, where the armistice terms had been dealt out to Germany at the close of World War I. Just previous to the closing of hostilities in France, Italy had declared war on France and was now committed as an Axis power.

Hotchkiss H35 37mm

Far left, destroyed French H-35. Left, German inspecting captured French S-35 tank (Warpics). Above, German PzKpfw. IV/D of 5th Panzer Div. (Odell)

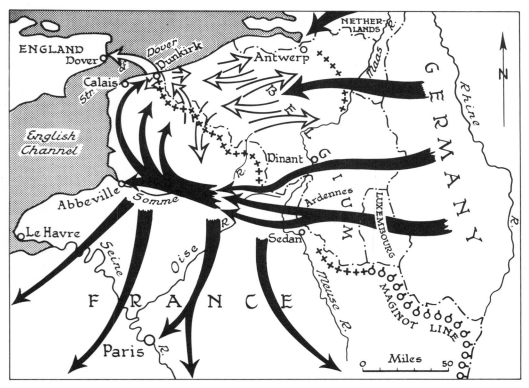

Germany first applied pressure in the north, then drove an armored wedge between northern and southern forces, encircling the B.E.F. They then drove south to complete the victory.

OPERATION SEA LION: With the fall of France, Germany looked across the channel to Britain. If they could command control of the air and ensure enough shipping to transport the appropriate land forces, the German High Command felt confident that England would surrender and bring an end to the war. In preparation for these landings, underwater tanks were being developed and tested in Holstein. Both PzKpfw. III and IV were fitted with long snorkeling devices which were to feed air to the tanks while they crawled along the floor of the channel. The tanks were to be launched in the proper depth of water just off the coast and would make their way ashore along the bottom. When it became obvious that neither the air supremacy nor the required number of landing craft could be achieved, the whole operation was canceled. However, the underwater training would prove worthwhile in 1941 when these same tanks were used in the opening phase of the Russian offensive and crossed under the Bug River.

After the French campaign, Hitler ordered a considerable increase in the number of Panzer and motorized infantry divisions. On paper the roster of Panzer divisions was doubled by halving the tank strength of each existing unit, while the motor vehicle industry was instructed to swing into full production to fill the gap in vehicles. Much captured equipment was also put into service at this time.

ITALY INVADES GREECE: Although the Italians had clashed with British forces in Libya and Somaliland, Mussolini could boast of no victories paralleling Hitler's. Striking out from Albania on October 28, an Italian army of 162,000 men advanced into Greece with the intention of overrunning the country and threatening British bases in the eastern Mediterranean. Although poorly equipped, the Greek army forced the Italians well back into Albania. Mussolini rushed reinforcements to Albania, but the Greek advance continued. Before they could be stopped the Greeks were in control of one fourth of the country. Finally the Italians massed enough troops to withhold

Greek advances and force a stalemate along the whole front. At this point Hitler was looking toward the Balkans with an eye to securing his flank when he made his move against Russia. In an attempt to do this through diplomacy rather than taxing his armies more than necessary, he laid an ultimatum before Hungary, Rumania, Bulgaria, and Yugoslavia-three decided to join the Axis. Yugoslavia, however, resisted the threat and was to pay a heavy price the following spring. At this point in the war, Britain was building up its forces in Egypt to ward off the mammoth Italian army of Marshal Graziani and was able to dispatch only token troops to assist the Greeks.

British Attack Italians in Egypt

Italian L 3/35 light tank *(IWM)*

British A13 cruisers used
against the Italians *(IWM)*

In mid-September Graziani had sent his tanks and motorized divisions across the Egyptian border, forcing the light British forces back to Mersa Matruh. With an overwhelming superiority of 300,000 men against 70,000 British troops, and a greater number of tanks, guns, anti-tank weapons and planes than his foe, Graziani unaccountably halted at Sidi Barrani for three months. During this period Britain reinforced General Wavell's forces with better tanks plus Australian, North African, Indian, and New Zealand troops. On December 6, in a surprise attack, using his A13 cruisers and the heavy Matilda Mk. II Infantry tanks, Wavell took the offensive. The plan was to sweep inconspicuously around the Italian southern defenses and lay up in hiding the better part of the following day. This move was undetected by the Italians, and at dawn on December 9 the 7th Royal Tank Regiment struck at Nibeiwa Camp. The enemy was completely overwhelmed when their anti-tank weapons proved useless against the thick-skinned Matildas. The twenty-three Italian M11 tanks in camp were knocked out within ten minutes. Four thousand prisoners were taken at a cost of seven British dead.

Tobruk and Benghazi Fall to the British

Meanwhile, the 4th Armored Brigade struck north and cut the coast road, severing the main route of retreat. On the following day 2,500 prisoners and 100 guns fell to the British at Sidi Barrani. General O'Connor then sent the 7th Armored Brigade in a rapid move to Buq Buq, twenty miles west along the coast. Here again 14,000 surprised Italian troops were put in the bag. The British continued to sweep around Italian positions and plug retreat routes. Bardia was soon isolated and was assaulted on January 3 by the 6th Australian Division supported by Matildas of the 7th Royal Tank Regiment. On January 5, 40,000 men, 127 tanks and 462 guns were surrendered to the British forces. Tobruk and its garrison of 25,000 men fell to the 6th Australian Division supported by 16 tanks on January 22. Booty included 87 tanks and 208 guns. At this point the Matilda was the queen of the battlefield, figuring significantly in all these victories. After a historic dash across the desert to isolate Benghazi, the British intercepted the Italian armor at Beda Fomm and destroyed over 100 Italian M13's in a bitter fight. An entire Italian Army had been lost.

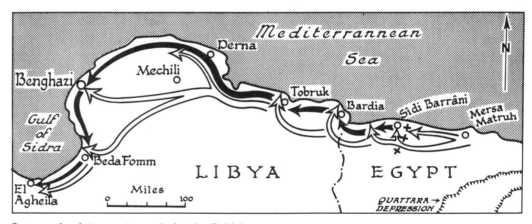

Successive intercepts made by the British.

Captured Italian M11/39 tanks *(IWM)*

Germans Sweep to Greek Border

With Hungary, Rumania and Bulgaria at his disposal, Hitler immediately began his preparations for the invasion of Yugoslavia and Greece. By March 2 German armor was on the Bulgarian-Greek border in readiness for the sweep south to Thessaloniki. Yugoslavia, in the meantime, decided to sign the Axis pact, but an overthrow of the government scrapped it. All these developments began to worry Britain, and to help protect her Mediterranean bases in Greece she hurriedly recalled about 60,000 troops from Africa, where they had just won their great victory over the Italians. A9 and A10 cruiser tanks were about all the British could spare for Greece.

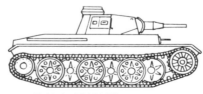

PzKpfw III/IV 50mm

Far left, German PzKpfw. II with 20 mm gun, fording a river. Left, PzKpfw. III/E with 50mm gun

Rommel Strikes in North Africa

The Afrika Korps had arrived in Libya in March, and after quickly surveying the situation Rommel felt sure that he could move against the forward British positions at El Agheila. What started off as a probe turned into a thrust in depth. By April 3 Rommel had taken Benghazi and was already directing an armored sweep across the desert wastes to intercept the retreating British at Mechili and Derna. By the tenth he had rolled past the garrison at Tobruk and was in Bardia three days later. Tobruk, however, continued to act as a thorn in Rommel's side, and although it was assaulted several times it remained firmly in British control.

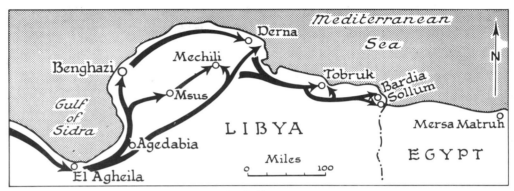

Rommel's rapid advances throughout April 1941

PzSpw(Sd.Kfz 231) 20mm

Far right a German SdKfz. 231 eight-wheeled armored car. Right, German PzKpfw. III being unloaded in North Africa

British Evacuate Greece & Crete

On April 6 Hitler struck at both Yugoslavia and Greece. German spearheads quickly joined up with the Italians, and together they drove the Greek armies back. With an air superiority of ten to one, the German columns soon drove a wedge between the Greeks and the British, forcing the Greek Army to surrender. The British retreated fighting a series of rear-guard actions. British armor was continually plagued with breakdowns and thrown tracks; what few pieces did make the long trek back to evacuation points had to be left behind. Over 50,000 troops were rescued in a desperate race through a German air umbrella, and although lacking their heavy equipment, were landed in Egypt to help stem off Rommel's advance. The American M3 Honey was waiting to re-equip many of the armored units. After the evacuation, German paratroopers were dropped into Crete followed by troop carrier aircraft to seal the fate of this last parcel of Greece.

German PzKpfw. III column enters Thessaloniki *(IWM)*

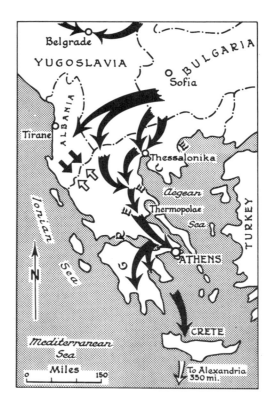

The British retreat and evacuation of Greece and Crete.

"Operation Barbarossa" – Hitler Attacks Russia

Hitler had been warned by many of his top generals that opening a second front in the east before the war with England was fully decided would be a dangerous act. Germany and Russia were on reasonably good terms at this time, and considering Russia's numerical superiority in men and tanks, it looked like a very hazardous undertaking. However, early on June 22, three great Army Groups moved forward on a 1,500 mile front from the Baltic to the Black Sea. These were Army Groups North, Center and South, under Field Marshals Leeb, Bock and Rundstedt, respectively. The plan was to strike hard and deep with the armored formations in order to isolate and destroy the Russian armies before they could regroup.

German PzKpfw. III/F advancing with infantry support. National flag wrapped around the stowage bin provided easy air identification

PzKpfw III(F,G,H) 50mm

British Open Offensive in Libya

Pressure from London had prodded Wavell into launching "Operation Battleaxe," even though his build-up was not completed. The attack opened on May 15 but immediately encountered heavy resistance. Captain Bach's concealed 88-mm guns at Halfaya Pass played havoc with the British armor, the first of many instances when this weapon proved the deliverance of Rommel's forces. The British managed to squeeze through to Capuzzo and the Sollum area, and it was hoped that the garrisons from Tobruk would be able to bring pressure to bear on Rommel's rear. However, they were repelled repeatedly by counterattacking German armor which neatly outflanked them and cut their supply routes. After three days of battle, Wavell was forced to acknowledge defeat and withdrew the remnants of his forces into Egypt. The new Crusader tanks made their first appearance in this battle but proved to be far too lightly armored and armed. The Matilda II infantry tanks still withstood enemy tank fire, but were too slow for the fast-flowing battle at which the Germans excelled. In its anti-tank role, the German 88 had neutralized the British reliance on the Matilda's heavy armor protection.

A captured British Matilda I with the 2 pounder (40mm) main armanent

Ukraine Falls to Germany

Initial successes of the German advance were nothing less than spectacular. As in France, their whole tank strength was concentrated in the Panzer divisions, which in turn were grouped into Panzer corps, and these corps into Panzer armies. At the commencement of this onslaught the Germans had some 5,264 tanks of all types, not including captured French vehicles. Of these, about 3,350 tanks, including most of their 1,440 PzKpfw. III and 517 PzKpfw. IV models, were thrown into the Russian offensive. To counter these the Russians had from 20,000 to 24,000 tanks of all types, although only a portion of these were at the front initially. However, German tank tactics enabled them to defeat this numerically superior force, and during the first five months they destroyed or captured about 17,000 Soviet tanks with a loss of 2,700 of their own. However, even this loss greatly hampered German strength on such a vast front.

German PzKpfw. 35(t) supporting infantry advance *(Odell)*

Destroyed Russian T26 light tanks

Russians Continue to Withdraw

In the first month the Germans drove ahead from 200 to 400 miles all along the Russian front. Bock was particularly successful on the central front, where, after capturing vast numbers of prisoners in battles at Minsk and

Above, the Russian T-28 heavy tank
Below, a disabled Soviet BT-5 *(Warpics)*

Smolensk, he was two-thirds of the way to Moscow. The Russians, however, continued to withdraw, regroup, and oppose these advances with a seemingly unending source of reserves. Although Russia had produced more tanks than all other countries of the world combined, she had concentrated on mass production of T-26, T-28, B. T. and T-35 types, which, although well armed, were close to being obsolete. To make matters worse, she had just decided to reorganize her armored forces on more effective lines. At the time of the German attack, Russia was caught off balance in this realignment. However, the new T-34 was beginning to appear in service and came as a surprise early in the campaign. It proved superior to anything the Germans could muster,

both in armament and armor. The sharply sloped glacis plate and overhanging hull of the T-34 were destined to influence tank design for many years to come. The KV heavy with its 76-mm gun, and the KV2 monster with a 122-mm gun in its box-like turret, were also encountered in small numbers. The German High Command hoped to concentrate on the central front and send Bock's tanks crashing through to Moscow, thus destroying Russia's nerve center. But Hitler had other plans. He was anxious to capture Leningrad and also to seal off Russia's oil supplies from the Caucasus. This decision to shift his forces away from the central push became the deciding factor that saved Moscow from being occupied before winter set in.

Winter Halts the Drive on Moscow

In late September, after Bock had assisted Rundstedt in capturing 600,000 Russian prisoners in a tremendous battle of encirclement near Kiev, Hitler finally allowed the drive on Moscow to recommence. During the brief relief of German pressure the Russians had set up strong defenses before Moscow and found the reserves to man them. Now, in October, the fall rains and muddy roads and fields hampered German armor movements. By mid-October Moscow was being attacked from three sides and all essential industry and Soviet officials were evacuated. Stalin, however, remained to direct the battle. By December 5 German advance units were in the outskirts of the city, but stiff resistance combined with freezing weather and snow stopped them in their tracks.

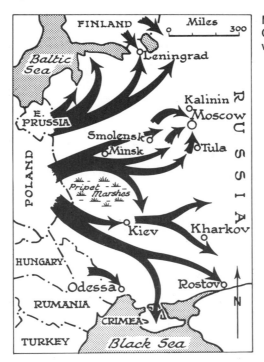

Vehicles and weapons froze. Troops were forced to carry on without the promised winter clothing. The Russians, on the other hand, were prepared for the snow and pushed the German forces back.

Map depicts basic advances of Army Groups North, Center, and South, all of which fell just short of their objectives.

The multi-turretted Russian T-35 heavy tank was no match for the faster and more maneuverable German Panzers

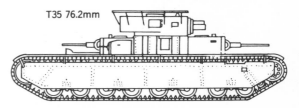

T35 76.2mm

Auchinleck Launches "Operation Crusader"

With an air superiority of three to one, General Auchinleck was able to muster his formations without being observed by Rommel's long-range reconnaissance planes. When British armored brigades streamed northward across the frontier wire at Fort Maddalena and took up battle positions on the Trigh-el-Abd, Rommel was taken completely by surprise.

This was a battle where confusion reigned supreme, and the initiative swayed constantly back and forth. The Eighth Army had 455 tanks against Rommel's 412. The plan of attack involved feints from the south and central regions while the main attack was a direct thrust towards Tobruk. The first objective was the destruction of the 15th and 21st Panzer Divisions which were the backbone of the Afrika Korps. The heart of the battle was Sidi Rezegh, the key to Tobruk. Over this barren air strip were strewn disabled aircraft and tanks from both sides. Sidi Rezegh Ridge changed hands several times within as many days. Contact was made with the Tobruk garrison, and then broken again. Communications within the 4th Armored Brigade broke down completely when their Headquarters was captured accidentally by the 15th Panzer. Similarly, on the following day the New Zealanders captured Headquarters Afrika Korps, but both Rommel and General Cruewell were in the field at the time. Finally Rommel initiated a deep thrust into the British rear areas with the hope of strangling the British armor in its forward positions.

M3 Stuarts, christened "Honeys" by the British crews

At first the British rear began to collapse, but Auchinleck refused to be bluffed and struck in retaliation at Rommel's exposed rear. Realizing that the ruse was not working, Rommel broke off this advance into Egypt. Contact had been made with Tobruk again, and Sidi Rezegh once more turned into a battlefield. Rommel, with a brilliant combination of tanks and anti-tank guns, managed to thwart every move the British armor tried to make. However, the stiff fighting soon began to tell on the German strength, and after a final attempt to inflict a decisive defeat on British armor on December 6 and 7, Rommel withdrew to a line running south from Gazala. On the thirteenth the British attacked this line, but it was not decisive and Rommel again withdrew, this time to return all the way back to the El Agheila defenses. The British 7th Armored was sent in hot pursuit across the intervening desert but failed to cut off this withdrawal.

Burning PzKpfw. III being inspected by crew of a British Crusader

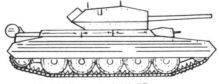

Mk.VI "Crusader" III 57mm

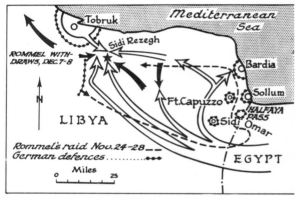

Operation "Crusader" — November 1941

Disabled PzKpfw. III/H

Japan Attacks Pearl Harbor

RUSSIA COUNTERATTACKS: On December 5, the Russian forces under General Zhukov, accompanied by numbers of T-34 tanks, launched a counterattack against Bock's forces. The T-34 excelled in the snow-covered terrain and the Germans were forced to withdraw and form a defensive line some 50 to 100 miles back from Moscow. In the south, Marshal Timosheko also recaptured the city of Rostov.

PEARL HARBOR: Japan had been playing a gradual game in Asia — conquering portions of China and French Indochina and slowly closing in on the British and Dutch colonies in the Pacific. America's reaction was to cut off trade with Japan and eventually the Allies froze all Japanese assets. Realizing that she would soon be strangled and weakened by these moves, Japan prepared for a swift and short war with the United States. The Japanese fleet slipped quietly to a point north of Hawaii and on the morning of the December 7 launched 353 planes in an attack against Pearl Harbor with the hope of destroying the bulk of the U.S. Fleet. Fortunately, the U.S. carriers were not in port, but damage to the fleet was still severe.

Early model Soviet T34/76 on reconnaissance *(Sovfoto)*

Japanese Advance in Malaya

On the same day as the Pearl Harbor attack the Japanese also landed amphibious assault forces in Malaya and Thailand. From Singapore, Britain sent the battleships *Prince of Wales* and *Repulse,* plus four destroyers, to intercept these troop transports and landing craft. Without air cover these huge ships were easy prey for the Japanese torpedo and dive bombers, and both were sent to the bottom. General Yamashita's troops struck down both sides of the Malay Peninsula toward Singapore. Properly outfitted and skilled in jungle warfare, the Japanese easily infiltrated and outflanked the bewildered British and Australian troops. Japanese tanks of the 3rd Division forged down the main roads against moderate British resistance.

Japanese Type 95 light tanks disabled during the fighting in Malaya. Note MG mounting in rear of turret *(IWM)*

Type 95 "Kyu-go" 37mm

Rommel Strikes Again

German PzKpfw. IV moves forward *(Odell)*

Rommel had fallen back to a very resistant defensive position at El Agheila, and until Auchinleck overpowered the Axis forces left behind at Bardia and Sollum, he was unable to apply enough pressure to break it. These two fortresses held out until January 17 and during this time German air power concentrated on neutralizing Malta to ensure that war shipments got through to Rommel. Supplies arrived safely during January, enabling Rommel to quickly rebuild his army. He now had 139 German and 89 Italian tanks at his disposal, and on January 21, just a fortnight after his retreat, Rommel's forces once again leapt forward on a drive that was to carry him within sixty miles of Alexandria. Not prepared for any sudden reversals of this nature, the Eighth Army was unable to stop Rommel's initial move. Orders were given to form a strong defensive line at Gazala, about 40 miles west of Tobruk. During his rapid advance, Rommel succeeded in capturing a number of British fuel and equipment dumps before they could be destroyed. With this captured material he was able to feed and re-equip his army without pausing. Before the end of January he had captured Benghazi and its British garrison. Continuing along the coastal road, and also cutting across the inland desert, his forces reached Auchinleck's new defensive positions on February 4. Although the British defenses were weak, Rommel had outrun his supplies and was forced to pause and regroup. Both sides built up their strength feverishly. At this point Rommel's main battle tanks were still 223 PzKpfw. III with the short barreled 50-mm gun, although nineteen of the new long barreled variety had arrived. As for the PzKpfw. IV, all forty carried short barreled 75's except for four long barreled models whose ammunition had not yet arrived. There were also fifty PzKpfw. II's and 228 Italian M13/40 and M14/41's at Rommel's disposal. Soon, however, he was to encounter the American-made M-3 Medium with its long range 75-mm gun, which only his 88-mm anti-tank guns could match.

A semi-tracked German 20mm Flak gun *(IWM)*

Japanese Capture Singapore

Japanese Type 94 TK tankettes towing tracked supply carriers *(IWM)*

Japanese landing forces pushed ashore day and night onto the Malay Peninsula. In many cases new beachheads were formed behind defending British forces, cutting them off from their line of retreat. By early February the British troops had been forced back to Singapore. On February 15, sixty-nine days after the Japanese first landed on the Malay Peninsula, Singapore, supposedly the strongest naval base in the world, had surrendered. The fact that it had been attacked by land forces from the peninsula rather than by sea accounted for its downfall.

Type 94 MG

Close of Winter on the Eastern Front

Throughout the bitter Russian winter the Germans had held on desperately to their positions despite constant Soviet pressure. On March 24 the Germans launched their biggest attack on the Kalinin front since the Battle of Moscow. The object was to relieve troops that had been isolated in the Rzhev area. Three divisions with heavy tank support were thrown into the attack, but after five days of fruitless fighting they had to withdraw. Meanwhile, near Staraya they were also attempting to relieve the 16th Army, which by now had been reduced to almost half strength. The Russians too were battering away at Leningrad in an attempt to free the isolated city before the spring thaws cut their only supply link across the frozen surface of Lake Ladoga. And in the Ukraine the Soviets had reached the suburbs of Stalino, which they had lost the previous October, and were fighting desperately to regain the town. The German soldier had spent an utterly miserable winter and frostbite had taken almost as heavy a toll as the Russian attacks.

German infantry advances behind a PzKpfw. III. Note the extra stowage bin attached to rear deck (Odell)

PzKpfw III 50mm

Japs Speed Ahead in Burma

Burma and the Dutch Indies had also been attacked in mid-January. The Dutch East Indies provided Japan with great treasures of oil, rubber, quinine and other strategic products. The Japanese had driven through Burma routing all British, American, and Chinese troops from the country. However, General Stilwell managed to extricate the bulk of his U.S. troops from Burma by marching them through 110 miles of jungle to India, after they had lost all their heavy equipment. By May 1 the Japanese had forced all British troops out of Burma and sealed off the Burma Road supply line to China.

Antiquated M-89/B, one of the models put into service by the Japanese in early WW II campaigns.

Germans Launch Caucasus Push

With spring, Hitler once again fixed his eyes on the Caucasian oil fields, and even dreamed of joining hands with Rommel in the Near East. Stalingrad also fell into his picture. On May 8 Field Marshal Manstein opened his offensive against the seaport area of Kerch in the Crimea. Four days later, Timoshenko, in an attempt to upset German plans, attacked Kharkov from the south. The Germans counterattacked and threw the Russians back with heavy losses. On May 23, the Russians evacuated the Kerch Peninsula and the German right flank was secured. Eventually this southern offensive was destined to end in disaster for the Germans when the 6th Army was ordered to hold its extended position at Stalingrad after it had been encircled by the Russians.

German Sturmgeschutz III mounting a fixed short-barrelled 75mm gun. This was an assault vehicle based on the PzKpfw. III chassis *(Odell)*

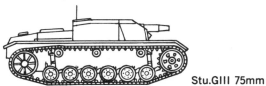

Stu.GIII 75mm

Rommel Moves In on Tobruk

The British had built up a powerful line of fortifications for forty miles inland from Gazala, on the coast, to Bir Hacheim. It consisted of a series of entrenchments with deep mine-fields covering the front and each strong point. On the night of May 26 Rommel ordered his Italian troops to attack all along this front, while he personally led the 21st and 15th Panzer, plus the 90th Light Division and Italian Ariete, south around Bir Hacheim and up into the British rear. The 90th Light shot out for El Adem, and the armor struck north for Knightsbridge, encountering the 4th Armored Brigade in the process. Here, the Germans met their first M-3 Grant tanks and were seriously mauled. The 15th Panzer lost some 100 vehicles in the encounter. By the twenty-eighth, Rommel's supply lines from the south were penetrated and he was forced to clear supply lanes through the mine fields. Heavy fighting continued in the "Cauldron," but by June 1 the box at Got el Ualeb had fallen and Rommel turned the 90th Light and the Trieste against Bir Hacheim. After fierce resistance by Free French and Jewish troops, Bir Hacheim was evacuated by night. This final thorn in Rommel's back had been removed. Once more he seized the initiative and continually lured British tanks into his ambushes of 88-mm guns. By June 13 the British had only some sixty-five tanks left of their original 849, which had consisted of 167 Grants, 149 Stuarts, 257 Crusaders, 166 Valentines and 110 Matildas. The Germans, moreover, claimed the battlefield and utilized the recovered vehicles.

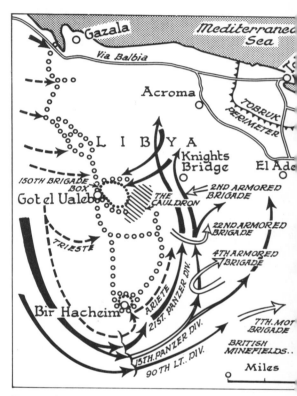

Rommel turns the Gazala Line

Tobruk Falls

Rommel now threw everything he had against Tobruk. With supporting Stukas clearing a path through the heavy minefields, he quickly broke into the first line of defense from the southeast. His main ruse was to bypass Tobruk with his armor and advance instead on Bardia to suggest to the British defenders that he once again intended to press on without besieging Tobruk. However, during the night of June 19 this force turned back, and when the dive bombers appeared at dawn the whole Afrika Korps was there to follow up. The British garrison of thirty thousand men was still exhausted from previous battles, and morale was much lower than it had been in 1941. Sappers bridged the tank traps with empty oil drums, and with one huge push the Germans were inside the main defenses and advancing on the city. Large quantities of fuel and supplies were captured with the defenders.

Italian Semovente 75/18 75mm assault gun beefed up with spare tracks and sandbags *(IWM)*

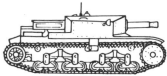

Semovente 75/18 75mm

German SdKfz. 251/3 (FU) halftrack operating with a towed artillery unit of the 21st Pz. Division *(Odell)*

Rommel Strikes Out for Cairo

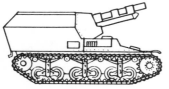

Gw.Lr.S 150mm

With hardly a breather, Rommel put his tired troops in hot pursuit of the disorganized British forces retreating along the coastal road toward Mersa Matruh and beyond. Cairo was in complete panic and exaggerated reports added to the confusion. Fighting a skillful delaying action, and supported by all the air strikes he could muster, Auchinleck managed to restore order to the shattered Eighth Army. With the time gained, he built up a strong defensive line stretching from El Alamein south to the impassable Qattara Depression. Rommel reached and probed this line late in June, and by July 7 his full force was opposite the El Alamein line. It was obvious that this was a formidable obstacle for his depleted Panzer divisions. The German supply line at this stage stretched all the way back to Benghazi and was under constant air attack, while the Eighth Army hauled its replacements right out of the Suez Canal.

The German heavy self-propelled howitzer "Lorraine Schlepper," a number of which were fed into the El Alamein offensive. It carried a Krupp 15cm gun mounted on the captured French Tracteur Blinde 38L chassis *(IWM)*

Germans Capture Sevastopol

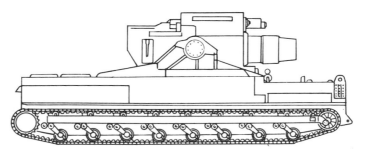

The 600mm Heavy Siege Mortar "Karl" (Gerat "040")

On the southern flank of the German offensive into Russia was the fortress of Sevastopol in the Crimea. Through this naval base the Russians could still dominate the Black Sea and its coastal waters. On June 3 Manstein launched the opening aerial bombardment and the long thirty day battle against the world's strongest fortress began. A massive mortar barrage, consisting of 576 barrels, poured mortar bombs into the holocaust at a rate of 324 per second. Among this troop towered the Karl (or Thor) self-propelled 600-mm siege mortar. This was the first of six eventually built, the later five being equipped with interchangeable 540-mm barrels. It weighed in the neighborhood of 125 tons and launched 2-1/4 ton concrete-piercing bombs which shattered even the strongest roofs. It was supported by modified PzKpfw. IV ammunition carriers which hoisted the projectiles into firing position. Unable to withstand the pressure, Sevastopol finally fell on July 3, 1942.

Russians Lose Rostov

Rostov became the next main point of resistance, and once Voroshilovgrad to the north was taken the Germans surged into the Lower Don basin. Since its recapture, Rostov had been heavily fortified with three defensive skirts of deep mine fields and anti-tank obstacles. Even so, assault groups of LVII Panzer Corps managed to breach the outer lines in a surprise attack. The 4th Panzer Regiment broke in from the north and SS Panzer Grenadier Division "Viking" struck through numerous strong points and anti-tank ditches to seize the airfield. Vicious street fighting ensued with the NKVD snipers fighting to their last bullet, but by July 27 the LVII Panzer Corps was moving south across the Don on its way to the Caucasus.

The mammoth Russian KV2 mounting a 152mm howitzer was basically unsuccessful because of its excess height and clumsy design

KV2 152mm

Germans Advance into Caucasus

Although Hitler's plan to strike out for both Stalingrad and the Baku oil fields in the Caucasus was considered foolhardy by his generals, it progressed well until the troops and equipment were stretched beyond their resources. At this point both offensives began to bog down, and the Russians started preparations to take advantage of the situation. By enticing the Germans into the wide open spaces of Russia they were able to dilute the effect of the armored spearheads. South of the Don lay three hundred miles of open steppe with limited water supplies, backed by a mountain range. It proved ideal for defense and soaked up much of the materiel required for a decisive German victory in the plunge against Stalingrad. The oil fields at Baku were never quite reached, although the Germans exhausted themselves trying.

German PzKpfw. III tank
supports infantry advance

The German drive into the Caucasus
fell short of the rich Baku oil fields

Canadians Raid Dieppe

On August 19 a force of 4,693 Canadians, plus British commandos and fifty U.S. Rangers, landed on the beaches at Dieppe. All these men had been itching to get into action after two years of maneuvers in England. But the mission seemed doomed from the start. The supporting Churchill I, II and III tanks that were landed from LCT's were unable to find traction on the rounded, smooth stones of the beach, and most ended up as sitting ducks for the German artillery. Many tanks were drowned, and twenty-eight Churchills were left for the Germans to inspect; 2,851 men were killed or captured. Several tanks did manage to break through the beach defenses and into the town, but on the whole the mission was a disaster. Although

Low tide photo showing the Churchills immobilized on the pebble beach *(DND)*

it convinced the Allies that overpowering naval bombardments must accompany amphibious landings, it also prodded the Germans into improving their defenses.

Rommel Attacks the El Alamein Line

On the night of August 30 Rommel made his move, having been assured that the required fuel for his Panzer thrust would be delivered to him by airlift if necessary. Aided by diversionary raids in the north and center, Rommel launched an enveloping attack in the south and managed to break through. A concerted thrust at the strongly defended Alam Halfa Ridge was partially successful, but lack of fuel and the persistent British aerial attacks brought it to a halt. On September 1 the 15th Panzer moved out again and, although suffering greater losses, managed to come out on top of a battle with the 8th Armored Brigade. Rommel could see that he was getting nowhere and ordered a general withdrawal under incessant RAF attack. Attempts were made by the British 7th Armored to

cut the Germans off, but although bitter fighting took place they were unable to accomplish the feat. Rommel had lost fifty tanks and thirty-five anti-tank guns in this venture and the British, sixty-eight tanks and eighteen anti-tank guns. For the Germans this equipment was almost impossible to replace.

Erwin Rommel

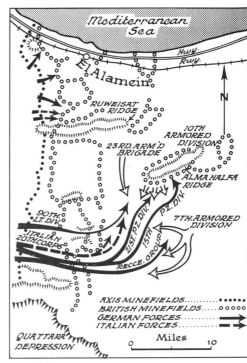

Rommel's vain attempt to break through the El Alamein defenses.

The El Alamein Offensive Begins

M-3 Grants on the move in the desert *(IWM)*

In the late evening of October 23, Montgomery unleashed a merciless artillery bombardment on the German-Italian defenses. By early morning of the twenty-fourth the leading elements of the British 1st and 10th Armored Divisions began to move through corridors in the German mine fields accompanied by troops of XXX and X Corps. This armored thrust soon bogged down in the tight mine field corridors. Montgomery decided to swing the 9th Australian Division north behind the German defenses in an attempt to isolate the enemy's northern salient and force Rommel to concentrate on its relief. Rommel had arrived back from Germany on the third day of the battle and at once realized that the situation was almost hopeless. His

German Counterattacks Fail

troops were outnumbered two-to-one and the armor was in even worse shape. He had 489 tanks pitted against 1,029 British armored vehicles. The German breakdown was eighty-five Mk. III's, eighty-eight Mk. III Specials, eight Mk. IV's, thirty Mk. IV Specials and 278 Italian M13/40 types. The British were able to muster 252 M4 Shermans, 170 M3 Grants, 294 Crusaders, 119 M3 Stuarts, and 194 Valentines, plus overwhelming air and artillery support. Bitter fighting ensued with Rommel gradually pulling his faithful 15th and 21st Panzer Divisions northward. Heavy losses were dealt to both sides, but the Germans had nothing in reserve. In the fighting of October 27 the Panzer Divisions lost fifty tanks to the 1st Armored, while the RAF completely disrupted all supply

attempts by the Germans. The Australians continued to wedge their way into the German positions in the north, and Montgomery prepared to launch "Operation Supercharge" against Italian opposition if possible. In the early hours of November 2 a creeping barrage from 300 25-pounders and the corps' medium artillery paved the way for Supercharge. The infantry went in on a 4,000 yard front, and the armor followed up to consolidate, sustaining heavy anti-tank casualties. Rommel had received Hitler's directive to "stand fast," but after an initial attempt to comply he disregarded the order and did everything he could to withdraw the Afrika Korps from the clutches of the Eighth Army. He had lost nearly 200 tanks and armored vehicles in this heavy fighting.

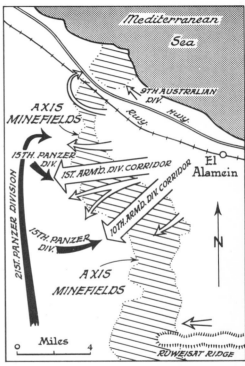

The German defenses proved no match for Montgomery's powerful all-out assault.

Rommel Is Forced To Retreat

By November 4 Rommel was in full retreat, with the Desert Air Force pounding him from above and the 1st, 7th and 10th Armored Divisions on his heels. Montgomery had hoped to bag the Afrika Korps in this initial battle, but it was always just out of his reach, and the arduous job of tracking Rommel all the way back to Tunisia had begun.

"Operation Torch" under the command of General Eisenhower had taken place on November 8, meeting light resistance at Casablanca, Oran, and Algiers. Upon learning of this, Rommel decided to retreat back to El Agheila, and by the thirteenth the advance guard of the Eighth Army was in Tobruk. By the twentieth they were in Benghazi, but Montgomery began to slow up the pursuit in order to reorganize and ensure supply.

Captured British equipment used by the Germans to alleviate their critical vehicle shortage. Left, a Humber A/Car. Right, a Matilda Infantry tank *(Odell)*

Russians Open Stalingrad Push

Although the Germans had reached Stalingrad in mid-August and practically leveled the city in their attempt to reach the Volga, by November they were still involved in bitter street and house-to-house fighting with the tenacious Russian defenders. With all the emphasis on capturing Stalingrad, the northern and southern flanks of this extended front had been neglected. On November 17 three Russian armies struck from the north and south, and in four days had cut off the German 6th Army. The immediate reaction of the German general staff was to have General Paulus break through this Russian barrier before it had time to build up. However, Hitler dictated that there

would be no withdrawal permitted, and Goering promised that the Luftwaffe would be able to supply the 300,000 troops in the pocket until ground forces broke through to relieve them.

Soviet troops on winter camouflaged T-34's. *(Sovfoto)*

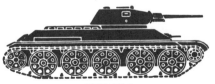

T34/76(B) 76.2mm

Major Armored Attacks of the Second World War

1 Polish Campaign:
September 1939

2 Battle of France:
May 1940

3 Battle of the Somme: June 1940

4 Sidi Barrani:
December 1940

5 Beda Fomm:
February 1941

6 Rommel's First Offensive into
Cyrenaica: April 1941

7 German Balkan Offensive:
April 1941

8 British "Operation Battleaxe":
June 1941

9 German "Operation Barbarossa"
Begins: June 1941

10 Battle of Kiev:
September 1941

11 German Southern Ukraine
Campaign: October 1941

12 German "Operation Typhoon,"
Battle of Moscow: October-
November 1941

13 British "Operation Crusader":
November 1941

14 Sidi Rezegh Battles:
November 1941

15 Soviet Winter Offensive:
December 1941

16 Rommel's Second Offensive into
Cyrenaica: January 1942

17 German Caucasus Offensive:
May 1942

18 German Gazala Offensive:
May 1942

19 Axis Siege of Bir Hacheim:
May 1942

20 "The Cauldron" Battles:
June 1942

21 German Siege of Tobruk:
June 1942

22 Rommel's Drive for Cairo:
July 1942

23 First Battle of El Alamein:
July 1942

24 German Caucasus Southern
Offensive: August 1942

25 Battle of Alam Halfa:
September 1942

26 Second Battle of El Alamein:
October 1942

27 Soviet Stalingrad Offensive:
November-December 1942

28 Soviet Kharkov Offensive:
January-February 1943

29 Battle for Kasserine Pass:
February 1943

30 Battle of Mareth:
March 1943

31 German Kharkov Counteroffensive:
March 1943

32 German "Operation Citadel,"
Battle of Kursk: June-July 1943

33 Conquest of Sicily:
July-August 1943

34 Soviet Smolensk Offensive:
August-October 1943

35 Salerno Beachhead:
September 1943

36 Battle of the River Sangro:
October 1943

37 Anzio Beachhead:
January 1944

38 Soviet Ukraine Offensive:
February-March 1944

39 British-Canadian Caen Offensives:
June-July 1944

40 Soviet Polish Offensive:
July 1944

41 Soviet Baltic States Offensive:
July-August 1944

42 American Breakout in Brittany:
August 1944

43 The Falaise Pocket:
August 1944

44 The Great Swan:
September 1944

45 Ardennes Offensive:
December 1944-January 1945

46 Soviet Offensive in East Prussia:
January 1945

47 Soviet Offensive in Poland & East
Germany: January-February 1945

48 Battle of the Rhine:
March-April 1945

49 Berlin Offensive:
April-May 1945

Rommel Withdraws from El Agheila

On November 26 the British had arrived at Rommel's El Agheila defenses, the third time they had been there in less than two years. There was still a slight fear that Rommel might have another ace up his sleeve with which to reverse the whole situation once more, but in truth he would never be able to launch another concerted attack in Cyrenaica. Montgomery decided to make sure that no reversal would occur and played all his cards carefully. In mid-December Montgomery sent the New Zealanders on a wide sweep south in an attempt to encircle the Panzer armies once and for all, but Rommel quickly withdrew and easily cut through these forces attempting to seal off the coastal road. Although finding the Via Balbia heavily mined

British Valentine tanks line up in Tripoli harbor

with tens of thousands of mines, the British advanced steadily and by December 29 were in contact with the Buerat defenses. By January 12, 1943, the build-up was complete, and air support available. Once again Monty tried an outflanking movement to the south with the 7th Armored, but the going was rough and the main thrust was diverted to the coastal highway. The Germans resisted again at Homs, but on January 23 the 51st Highlanders and 11th Hussars were in Tripoli.

Sixth Army Isolated at Stalingrad

Completely cut off, the men of the 6th Army under Paulus could do little more than wait for disaster to overtake them. The air supplies were far from adequate and soon the depletion of food and arms became acute. The Russians applied constant pressure to the perimeter and it was gradually squeezed smaller and smaller. By January 17 the Russians were within ten miles of the city proper, and recently promoted Field Marshal Paulus threw every man he had into the line, but in vain. Finally the remnants of this once great army were pinned in an oblong only four miles deep by eight miles long, and under intense artillery and air bombardment the final spasms of street fighting took place. On January 31 the surrender had begun. Of the 300,000 men of the twenty-one German divisions and the one Rumanian division originally trapped, only 90,000 survived the ordeal — and many of these would perish on their trek to the Russian camps.

Russian sweeps from north and south which isolated Sixth Army.

German armor in winter white. PzKpfw. III, PzKpfw. II, with a StuG III in the lead

In regaining Stalingrad, the Russians had quelled Germany's last hope of victory in that country. The vast quantities of men and equipment lost were irreplaceable, and the spirit of the German fighting man had been seriously undermined. All along the eastern front the Russians had taken a severe toll of German men and machines. Now, with their great resources of manpower and renewed production, they swept forward until by mid-February they had driven the Germans from the Kharkov area. Within a period of three months the Russians pushed forward over 430 miles west from Stalingrad.

Russian ski-troops towed by a T-34 and accompanied by a light T-26 *(Sovfoto)*

T-34's in winter camouflage moving forward in the winter drive *(Sovfoto)*

The extent of the Russian advance during their 1943 winter offensive. The map depicts the front as it appeared near mid-February

Battle for Kasserine Pass

The German position in the Tunisian bridgehead was reasonably vulnerable to an attack from the west which could divide the two Axis armies. In order to break up the American assembly areas in southwest Tunisia, Rommel chose to go on the offensive and dig deep into their positions at Gafsa and Faid Pass. On the fourteenth of February the 21st Panzer Division enveloped the 2nd U.S. Armored Division at Faid Pass and inflicted severe losses on the inexperienced American troops. However, the 21st Panzer hesitated to follow up this victory until February 16, and in the interval the Americans had prepared positions at Sbeitla which put up stiff resistance. The Gafsa positions had been evacuated because of the German advances to the north, and soon both German spearheads were zeroing in on Kasserine Pass. On the morning of February 20, the 21st and 10th Panzer Divisions plus elements of the 15th Panzer and Italian Ariete were massed before the pass on a seven-mile front. Artillery raged and the seasoned veterans of the Afrika Korps outshone the American armor crews. A number of German Tiger I tanks made their 88-mm guns felt, but although Rommel requested an additional nineteen which were with Arnim's 5th Panzer Army, he was refused. The 2nd U.S. Armored had lost in the neighborhood of 150 tanks, Shermans, and Lees, plus 1,600 men. The Americans seemed to be pulling back to Tebessa, and Rommel was all for making a deep strike now that things were moving so well. His choice of Tebessa as the target was not sanctioned and instead he was ordered to move north toward El Kef. Had Tebessa been taken, the Allies would likely have been forced to withdraw back into Algeria to regroup.

M-4 Sherman in Tunisia

M4A1"Sherman" 75mm

The terrain around Kasserine was very rugged and huge hilly sections proved ideal for the defending Americans. The accuracy of their artillery was devastating and managed to blunt the armored attack completely. By February 22 Rommel could see that this terrain was not suited for swift operations and, with the Americans and British throwing immense quantities of equipment into the gap, his weaker forces were obliged to withdraw. Signs also suggested that the Eighth Army was preparing to strike against the Mareth Line, which forced the decision to disengage. Rommel had severely punished the American troops and possibly postponed their planned offensive by nearly one month

Above, knocked-out M-3 Lee

U. S. M-3 Lee tank in Tunisia

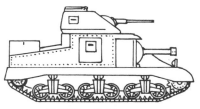

M3A5"Lee" 75mm

Refitted Shermans and
Grants returning to front

Eighth Army Reaches Mareth Line

As Rommel fell back through Libya from El Agheila, he had a two-front campaign on his hands. Montgomery's Eighth Army was approaching rapidly from the east and the Anglo-American First Army was applying pressure in the west. The Mareth Line was his last bastion of hope, and his attack at Medenine was his last offensive move with the Afrika Korps. Montgomery was aware that Rommel would attempt a delaying attack, and he had planted anti-tank defenses in concealed positions along his front. On the morning of March 6 Rommel watched his armor roll into position for the attack. The British guns were instructed to hold fire until the German armor was within 400 yards, and the results were deadly. British armor was held back and the heavy

attempt at infiltration by German infantry. Of the 150 German tanks employed, fifty-two were destroyed, while Montgomery withheld his total of 400 fit for action. By evening the artillery systematically crushed any

Germans drew off in confusion and Monty was free to pursue his calculated approach to the Mareth Line. Rommel relinquished his command for the last time and returned to Europe to report on the situation.

American-built Grant with
the British Eighth Army

Mk.III"Valentine"IV 40mm

Montgomery Breaks the Mareth Line

The main defenses of the Mareth Line utilized the formidable natural barrier of the Wadi Zigzaou. The 15th Panzer Division, with only fifty tanks, waited behind the Mareth, and the 10th Panzer had moved to Gafsa to watch the Americans. The 21st Panzer lay in reserve at Gabes with seventy tanks ready to support either front. Montgomery had decided to send his New Zealanders on a long left hook through the Matmata Hills to try and get behind the Mareth defenses. At the same time on the night of March 19 he sent his 50th Division against the Young Fascists near the coast in an attempt to bridge the anti-tank defenses in that area. With great effort the sappers managed to get forty Valentines across. On March 22 the 15th Panzer Division moved in and utterly destroyed this bridgehead. With this development Montgomery switched his attack to the Tebaga Gap where his 1st Armored Division swept through and immediately outflanked the Mareth Line. However, the Afrika Korps once again slipped through the noose and managed to form temporary defenses.

Germans Recapture Kharkov

The only spark of hope to appear for the Germans in the fighting on the eastern front in the early months of 1943 was Manstein's brilliant recapture of Kharkov. As the Russians moved steadily toward the Dnieper after taking Kharkov, Manstein launched a counterstroke which broke through their extended advance and threw them back in disorder. The feat was accomplished primarily with three divisions of the SS Panzerkorps, "Leibstandarte Adolf Hitler," "Das Reich" and "Totenkopf," using their Tiger tank battalions to best effect. This victory was to give Hitler false hopes for his planned summer offensive.

German Sturmgeschutz III Ausf. G used in infantry support and anti-tank roles *(IWM)*

Stu.G III 75mm

U.S. Forces Link with Eighth Army

By late April 1943 there was no more hope for Army Group Afrika. Overwhelming Allied air superiority had almost completely severed the air and sea supply lines from Sicily, and there were ever-increasing arrivals of materiel and manpower for the Allies. The British were moving on Tunis while the Americans zeroed in on Bizerte. In the extreme north the U.S. 9th Infantry Division, now under the command of General Omar Bradley, was making unexpected headway along the coast. Large-scale German withdrawals ensued, but the 9th was not equipped for rapid pursuit, and the U.S. 1st Armored remained bottled up in the "Mousetrap" until May 1 — thus permitting the Germans to make a rather orderly withdrawal through Mateur.

Captured German PzKpfw. III Ausf. N mounting the short 75mm gun *(IWM)*

PzKpfw III(N) 75mm

Tunis and Bizerte Fall to Allies

Early in May pressure was applied all along the First Army's front to avoid giving the Germans any respite. The main thrust came on May 5 with heavy aerial bombardments opening a path up the Medjerda valley for the British V Corps. Axis resistance completely crumpled under the pressure at some points, but at others the hardened Afrika Korps veterans put up a stiff fight. Massicault fell on the sixth, and on the following daybreak the 7th Armored Division struck out for Tunis. By early afternoon they had entered the city to the complete surprise of the occupants. At this point the Axis army in Tunisia was split into two parts. The British 6th Armored, which had more or less paralleled the 7th Armored, now swung southeast of the city to clean out Cap Bon Peninsula.

Shells being unloaded from M-3 Grant in preparation for complete overhaul.

Germans Surrender in North Africa

Tunis was totally subdued by May 8, and the British 7th Armored rolled out on a northerly route to meet up with the Americans coming south from Bizerte which they had occupied the day before. At this point the last refuge for the Germans was the Cap Bon Peninsula and some consideration was given to setting up defenses across that neck of land and attempting to hold out. This was hopeless however, and soon the Germans were marching into captivity under well-ordered discipline, and attempting to administer themselves until the Allies could set up proper prison facilities. The war in Africa had come to a close.

Captured Tiger I Ausf. E fitted for wading. In front is the NSU Kettenrad, with a PzKpfw. III/J in background *(IWM)*

PzKpfw VI"Tiger I"(E) 88mm

The Battle of Kursk

The Germans hoped that the Tiger I Ausf. E would once again give them the upper hand in battle, but even it could not stand up against broadside anti-tank fire *(Warpics)*

By the summer of 1943 the German forces were being pushed back on all fronts. In an attempt to regain the initiative in Russia and bolster the morale of the German people, "Operation Citadel" was put into effect. This plan involved massive armored thrusts from both north and south of the huge Kursk salient. Extreme care was put into the planning of this attack and every available piece of equipment was rounded up. For this attack the Germans had mustered 900,000 men, 10,000 artillery pieces and 2,700 tanks and assault guns. The new Tiger I, Tiger (P) Ferdinand and the medium Panther were to lead the way into what would prove to be the largest tank battle in history. However, Russian intelligence had learned of the impending attack on Kursk, and throughout the spring

"Operation Citadel"

months they had prepared powerful defensive lines on the Central and Voronezh fronts of the Kursk bulge. These were manned by 1,300,000 troops with 20,000 artillery pieces and 3,600 tanks and assault guns. In particular, the Soviets had concentrated much of their anti-tank artillery in this salient, and it was to take a great toll of German armor. Early in the morning of July 5 the battle began. From the north on the Orel-Kursk line, the German 9th Army under Col. General Model moved forward on a 25-mile front, with three Panzer and five infantry divisions. Forming the spearhead were about 500 tanks led by Tigers and Ferdinands in groups of ten to fifteen, followed by mediums in groups of fifty to one hundred. The well-emplaced Russian 76.2-mm anti-tank guns,

Armor-skirted PzKpfw. IV's move toward the battle area

T-34s and KV tanks fought them to a standstill in the course of four attacks throughout the day. In the southern section the attack did not go much better. From here Col. General Hoth's 4th Panzer Army consisting of five infantry, eight Panzer and one motorized division struck towards Oboyan. About 700 tanks took part

on this first day, with heavy air support, but the going was very rough. By the second day the main defensive belt had been penetrated. The Soviets had moved the 2nd and 5th Guards Tank Corps into prepared positions on the second belt and from here they pounded the German armor to a halt. In a final attempt to

Many Ferdinands fell prey to
Russian tank killers *(IWM)*
Above right, German StuG. III/G

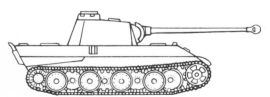

PzKpfw V"Panther" (D) 75mm

Formation of the new German medium Panther,
Ausf. D being prepared for action *(Odell)*

Destroyed Russian KV I

Russian T-34/76c destroyed by two broadsides.

T-34/76b with enlarged turret *(Warpics)*

save the situation the German command switched its main effort to Prokhorovka and threw in the best of their Waffen-SS Panzer forces. This involved 700 tanks led by 100 Tigers, aided by 300 tanks of Operational Group "Kempff" mounting a secondary attack from the south. At this point the Russian command decided it was time to move onto the offensive, and on July 12 the greatest tank battle in history took place in the Prokhorovka area. Here in the black clouds of battle some 1,500 tanks moved to meet each other head on. The Russian 5th Guards Tank Army cut completely through the German formations, and as the day wore on total confusion reigned. Firing was at point-blank range in many cases, and in this one day the Germans lost over 350 tanks and 10,000 officers

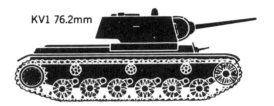

KV1 76.2mm

Russians Regain Kharkov

and men. The battle raged until late in the evening, but this was the turning point and the Germans never again acquired the initiative. They went over to the defensive and were eventually thrown into complete retreat. By July 23 they had withdrawn well beyond their start lines and it was obvious that Citadel was a disastrous failure. The Germans made desperate efforts to stop further Soviet progress and retain Kharkov, which was crucial to the defense of the Ukraine. Three Panzer divisions of the Waffen-SS, "Das Reich," "Totenkopf" and "Viking," were hurled against the Soviet 1st Tank Army south of Bogodukhov and the situation was momentarily saved. Kharkov was contested hotly but by August 23 the Germans began to pull out with the Red Army in full pursuit.

Russian KV I crewmen preparing for battle *(Sovfoto)*

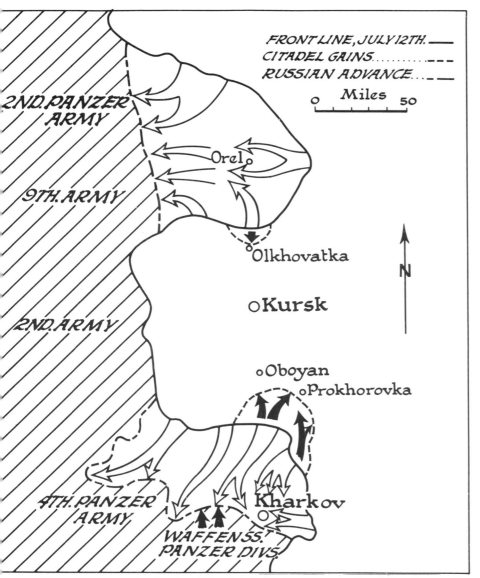

FRONT LINE, JULY 12TH. _____
CITADEL GAINS .... - - -
RUSSIAN ADVANCE... _ _

0 Miles 50

2ND. PANZER ARMY

9TH. ARMY

2ND. ARMY

Orel

N

Olkhovatka

o Kursk

o Oboyan
o Prokhorovka

4TH. PANZER ARMY

Kharkov

WAFFEN SS. PANZER DIVS.

The outcome of the Battle of Kursk left the Germans on the defensive again.

SICILY: In the Mediterranean, meanwhile, the Allies had landed in Sicily on July 10. The landings took the Axis completely by surprise. The Germans quickly recovered and launched stiff armored attacks that were beaten back only with the help of the large guns of the fleet off shore. Patton broke out to the north and west and within three weeks overran the whole western half of Sicily. Montgomery, however, ran up against a well-defended line anchored on Mount Etna, and it remained for Patton to outflank the Germans by amphibious landings along the north coast. By mid-August the Germans had completely withdrawn from Sicily and Messina was in Allied hands.

Allies Invade Italy

A Sherman tank of Canada's Calgary Regiment on a ridge overlooking Potenza, Italy, September 1943 *(DND)*

The Allied plan of attack on Italy was for Montgomery's Eighth Army to strike across the Messina Strait at the toe of Italy and thereby draw the German forces to the south. When this was effected, General Clark's U.S. Fifth Army would land at Salerno in the north in an attempt to cut into the German flank. The Germans had forseen this plan of action and at Salerno bitter resistance was met, which was only pushed back with the aid of the offshore naval batteries. By September 16 the Eighth Army had fought its way north to link with the U.S. Fifth and the slow procedure of ejecting the Germans from Italy had begun. Strong German defenses were set up behind the ideally located rivers. Foul weather brought the Allied advance to a crawl, while skillful rearguard actions by the withdrawing German 10th Army took a heavy toll of Allied lives.

By early December the drive for Rome had been completely halted before the vaunted defenses of the Gustav Line, where it would remain till the spring of 1944. The main difficulties thwarting advance in Italy were the numerous swollen rivers and the dominating heights of the Apennines which form the backbone of the Italian peninsula. From their lofty positions the Germans could bring down accurate fire on any Allied attempt to break through in the valleys below. With winter setting in, the cold, snow and ice added to the misery of the fighting men.

German crewmen adjusting track tension on their PzKpfw. IV *(Odell)*

Russians Reach Poland

By the close of 1943 the main German forces had been concentrated between the Pripet marshes and the Crimea. In order to outflank these armies the Russians chose to make a concerted effort on their first Ukrainian Front just south of the Pripet River. On December 24, after artillery and air bombardment, General Vatutin struck out against Manstein's 4th Panzer Army. Within five days a wedge 190 miles wide and 60 miles deep had been driven into Army Group South, with the result that the 1st Panzer Army was threatened with encirclement. The Germans answered this threat with a furious attack by five Panzer and four infantry divisions which suffered heavy losses but managed to halt the Russians.

However, by January 25 the Soviets were prepared for an all-out encircling offensive by the combined forces of the 1st and 2nd Ukrainian Fronts. The Germans, holding to their "no retreat" orders, were soon outflanked and by January 28 the ring had closed around the 1st Panzer Army. Over ten German divisions had been snared. While the German threat to their southern flank was still being nullified, the Russians struck through very difficult terrain north of the 4th Panzer Army and drove deep into pre-war Poland. This northern thrust left the German southern front precariously extended eastward, and soon it and the Crimea were to feel the full force of the Russian southern offensive.

Russian T60 light tank

T60 20mm

German PzKpfw. IV tanks
with supporting infantry

Anzio Beachhead

The Anzio landing was an attempt to break the deadlock which halted the Allied forces at the Gustav Line. It was intended to be a decisive outflanking attack, but as Churchill stated, "I had hoped we would be hurling a wildcat ashore, but all we got was a stranded whale." The landing began just before dawn on January 22, and although Field Marshal Kesselring was led to believe that the landings were intended for north of Rome, he soon had three divisions to intercept the cautiously advancing Allied VI Corps. By January 28 he had halted all Allied forward movement. By stripping additional units from the "Winter Line," France and the Balkans, the Germans prepared to launch eight divisions against the beachhead. In mid-February, with foul weather grounding the Allied air support, Kesselring launched an all out attack and very nearly broke through to the sea. However, the Allies held firmly, and with further reinforcements from the sea they managed to consolidate the landing. The battle now evolved into a complete stalemate and hopes of an outflanking movement were crushed. Only when the Gustav Line was pierced the following spring would the troops at Anzio once more be on the move.

(Sd.Kfz 251/22) 75mm

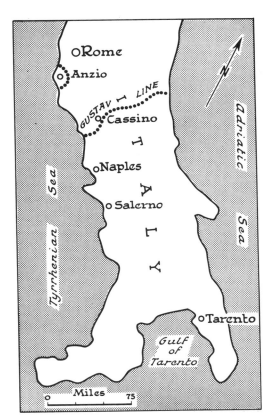

The stalemate at Cassino on the Gustav Line.

Red Army Sweeps Through the Ukraine

Spring came early in 1944, and with it the rising rivers and atrocious road conditions so prevalent in the Ukraine. The Russians, however, chose to keep up the pressure and doggedly continued their offensives. The Germans once again hoped that the heavy fighting of the previous months had drained the Russians of reserves, thus enabling the Germans to regroup their exhausted forces. Army Groups South and A could still muster eighty-three divisions and one brigade, including eighteen Panzer and four motorized divisions. To their dismay the Red Army attacked on all three Ukrainian Fronts. The 1st Ukrainian struck south in an attempt to cut off the withdrawal of German troops in the southern extension, while the 2nd and 3rd drove head-on toward Odessa and the Rumanian border. From the Pripet Marshes to the mouth of the Dnieper millions of men met in bitter conflict and soon the German defenses were broken all along the line. In an attempt to seal off the breakthrough at Uman the Germans committed their reserves. Hundreds of tanks and thousands of guns took part in the ensuing battle, but it ended in a Soviet victory. By March 24 Soviet armor had reached the Dniester, crossed it, and struck south to the Carpathian foothills. This sweep had cut through Army Group South and isolated the 1st Panzer Army. But before the ring could be strengthened the 1st Panzer regrouped and broke out using seven Panzer and three infantry divisions. The venture, however, cost them severely in men and heavy equipment.

Left, German anti-tank gunners attempting to stem the Russians *(Odell)*. Above, a Russian T34/76C *(IWM)*

In order to protect the northern flank of the 1st Ukrainian Front, the Soviets also made a thrust from their 2nd Belorussian Front through the almost impassable marshes and woods of the Pripet basin. By late March they had gained thirty to forty miles and had besieged Kovel. With all these northern advances by the Russians, the German southern armies had no choice but to withdraw.

The Red Army was closely pursuing them all the way and no opportunity was given to set up defenses on either the lower Bug or the Dniester rivers. In the extreme south the 3rd Ukrainian Front had used armor in night attacks and severely mauled the German 6th and Rumanian 3rd Armies. On March 8 the Soviets captured Novy Bug and struck south in an attempt to isolate the 6th Army.

Despite heavy losses the 6th managed to break through and reach the southern Bug, leaving behind its artillery and motor transport. The Germans attempted to set up defensive positions on the west bank of the southern Bug with the remaining twenty-one of their original thirty-four divisions, but by mid-March the Russians were across at Nikolayev, driving toward Odessa on the Black Sea.

Odessa and Sevastopol Fall

By early April the main front had moved far westward from the Crimea, but the Germans were determined to hold on there in an attempt to tie down Russian troops and interfere with the Black Sea fleet operations. The German and Rumanian forces consisted of 200,000 men, 3,600 guns and mortars and over 200 tanks and assault guns. Extensive anti-tank defenses stretched across the Perekop Isthmus. On April 8 the Russians unleashed a deadly bombardment against these defenses, and even before the artillery lifted, the Russian tanks and troops were upon the defenders. The main attack came in the Sivash sector rather than Perekop and caught the Germans by complete surprise. Two days of rugged fighting in rainy weather breached the defenses, and the Germans were forced to fall back to the fortifications of Sevastopol. During this period, Odessa had fallen and Sevastopol was now the last symbol of German resistance in the Crimea. After twenty days of careful planning the Russians feinted with their initial attack, and once the Germans had redeployed to meet it, struck home with their main force from the southeast on May 7. With guns massed at 320 per mile of front and heavy bomber attacks, they crushed the German defenses and then rammed their armor through. On May 9 defeat was complete.

The unrelenting Russian offensives in the early winter of 1944 eventually broke through to Rumania and Poland.

Allies Pierce the Gustav Line

For three months the Allies had pounded away at Monte Cassino defenses with little or no effect. First the Americans had tried, then the combined effort by French and American troops had failed, and finally an all-out effort by General Freyberg's New Zealanders was launched. None was able to break through the powerful German fortifications. Crack German paratroops held this position, and no amount of bombardment seemed able to unseat them. The air bombardment of the town of Cassino and of the hilltop monastery itself merely provided more rubble from which the paratroops could build stronger defenses. Finally, the Gustav Line was broken by a combined attack along the western coast. While the Eighth Army kept the Germans' occupied in the central region, the U.S. Fifth and the French forces broke through the main defenses in the plains to the west and soon threatened to outflank the Cassino positions. The Germans neatly pulled back before they could be cut off and hastily re-established on the Adolf Hitler line. However, pressure was too great and they were soon forced to abandon this position and fall back north of Rome. On June 4 the Allies marched into Rome.

A Sherman in the drive to Rome *(DND)*

D-Day– Allies Invade Europe

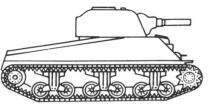

M4 "Sherman" 105mm

A Sherman BARV (Beach Armored Recovery Vehicle) passes a row of M-4 Shermans

Early on the morning of June 6 the long awaited assault against Hitler's vaunted "Fortress Europe" began. Before dawn, U.S. airborne troops drifted down into the areas to be exploited by the Utah Beach landings in an attempt to occupy the crucial crossroads and hinder German troop movements toward the beaches. To the east, the British 6th Airborne was assigned to occupy the bridge crossings on the Orne River and Caen Canal to permit the morning landings on Sword Beach to sweep inland on Caen. The story of the landings is well known and the amount of armor involved in the initial landings was minimal. However, the British and Canadians did launch the amphibious DD (Duplex Drive) Shermans in an attempt to get some heavy equipment ashore to support the infantry. Many of these vehicles never made it to shore because of the heavy seas. Of a group of thirty-two DD tanks launched from their tank-landing-craft 6,000 yards out, twenty-seven were swamped and sank within minutes. Most of these were meant for close support work with the engineers in breaching the initial German defenses. However, a number of LCT's managed to bring their tanks well in and these vehicles quickly waded ashore to give assistance to the infantry.

Canadian engineers preparing their beach for the heavy flow of traffic. *(DND)*

Light Mark VII Tetrarch *(IWM)*

The Normandy landings were supported by numerous specialized vehicles: flail-tanks for cutting mine-free exits from the beach, bridging-tanks to surmount the sea walls and ditches, petard-tanks to pulverize concrete obstacles, and BARV's to retrieve drowned tanks from deep shore waters. The petards and flails were kept busy clearing beach exits through the sea walls for the masses of tanks and other vehicles that had begun to build up on the beaches but were finding it difficult to break out and assist the already advancing infantry. Also involved in the D-Day landings were seven British-built Light Mk. VII Tetrarch airborne tanks. These were the first to go into action by air and were landed in Normandy by Hamilcar gliders as part of the 6th Airborne Division. One broke through the nose of its glider over the channel, but those that did survive the landing gave useful support as dug-in or mobile machine gun posts.

Cherbourg and Caen

Once the Normandy beachhead had been established, the Allies initiated the steps toward a final breakthrough. While the British and Canadian forces concentrated in the Caen area, the Americans made their move toward cutting the German line of retreat from the Cotentin Peninsula and securing the desperately needed port of Cherbourg. The sweep into the peninsula met determined anti-tank resistance in its early stages, but by June 21 the fortifications at Cherbourg were under siege. Directly inland from Omaha Beach in the St. Lô area, the U.S. armor found itself at the mercy of well-concealed German 88's as they struggled to advance through the bocage regions. Tanks were forced to follow the existing sunken road sys-

tems, and the German gunners had naturally prepared for this. During this time the British and Canadians continued to draw the bulk of the German armor to the Caen sector. Montgomery came under strong criticism for his slow and calculated advances, but his mind was made up. With Operation "Goodwood" he hoped to engage the German armor and "write it off." On July 18 the advance regiment of the 11th Armored Division moved through gaps in the minefield to follow up the scheduled aerial bombardment. They met little resistance as they followed a creeping artillery barrage, but after six miles of healthy progress they finally came under heavy flanking fire from well-emplaced 88's and Tigers of the 1st Panzer Division. Within

Right, Canadian Shermans move out for the final attack of "Operation Spring" (IW

minutes, a dozen British tanks were blazing. Some managed to reach the protection of the forward slopes of Bourguebus ridge, but the main body following met a rain of solid shot from the Panthers of the 1st SS Panzer Division which had attained the ridge above them and were picking off the hopelessly outgunned Shermans spread out below. On July 25, in conjunction with the American breakout "Operation Cobra," the Canadians, initiating "Operation Spring" were ordered to contain the German armor south of Caen. The attack went in during the dark under artificial moonlight, with bitter fighting. At dawn Panthers appeared on the left flank but a troop of 17-pounders accounted for four of them. The 7th Armored reported thirty enemy tanks hull-down between Fontenay and Rocquancourt. The Canadians were fought to a standstill, but this action had enabled the Americans to emerge into the open country beyond St. Lô.

Russians Burst Into Poland

In its third winter offensive of the war, the Red Army had pushed the Germans back almost to the Polish border. Now, as the Germans endeavored to strengthen their defenses, the Russians prepared for another onslaught. The 1st Ukrainian Front was equipped with eighty divisions; ten tank and mechanized brigades, totaling 1,200,000 men with 13,900 guns and mortars, 2,200 tanks and self-propelled guns and 2,800 aircraft. This was an armor superiority over the Germans (who had 900 vehicles) of 2.4 to 1. On July 13, with Brody as their objective, the Russians broke through the German defenses and by the third day armor was being fed through the gap. On July 17 the 1st Guards Tank Army was committed and that same day it crossed the Bug River. The 3rd and 4th Tank Armies had also gone in on other sectors. German defenses were completely shattered and their forces encircled in several instances. Lvov was soon captured and by July 27 the Vistula was in sight. Panzer battalions equipped with the King Tiger were rushed to the Vistula defenses but by early August the Russians were across it.

A disabled Russian KV I/A serves as cover for a German machinegunner (Odell)

Yanks Break Out into Brittany

On July 25, after massive air bombardments, Bradley's "Operation Cobra" struck out down the western edge of the Cotentin peninsula and within five days his armored spearheads had reached Avranches. It had been a slow start, but soon the armor was leaving the infantry behind and spreading utter chaos well beyond the German main defenses. Although Kluge extracted two Panzer divisions from Caen and directed them west to close the gap, they were neatly intercepted by the British Second Army and pinned down. The German left flank completely collapsed and by August 1 Avranches was an open gate for American forces streaming south, some turning west into Britany but the main force swinging east toward the eventual objective of the Seine. Patton's U.S.

Third Army was now given free rein to sweep south and east in a long-range plan to bottle up the German 5th and 7th Panzer Armies. Realizing this danger, and to avoid a withdrawal, Hitler ordered Kluge to throw his armor against Avranches in an attempt to sever the American supply route south. On August 7 four Panzer divisions surged through Mortain but bogged down under American resistance and overwhelming artillery fire. By evening, only thirty of Field Marshal Kluge's original seventy tanks were operational. Before these losses could be replaced, the Canadians struck with "Operation Totalize," driving over sixteen miles toward Falaise with 600 tanks. Hitler's dream was now down the drain and the German armies in France were close to being annihilated.

Falaise Pocket

German infantry take comfort in the presence of a late model Tiger I/E

Bradley could see that the Germans had incurred the risk of encirclement from both south and north and he instructed Major General Haislip's XV Corps to strike north for Argentan. Now everything evolved around closing the gap between Falaise and Argentan. On August 14 the Canadians and Poles struck on a narrow front to within three miles of Falaise, to leave a mere fifteen-mile corridor between the Allied armies. The pocket was now under heavy bombardment by air and artillery from all sides. On August 16 Falaise was finally under Canadian control and that night the German troops in the western end of the pocket began to withdraw. By the evening of August 19 the pocket was roughly six miles deep and seven miles wide. Inside were two army headquarters, plus the remnants of ten divisions.

Americans inspect
a disabled German
StuG. 40 Ausf. G

The Poles had managed to virtually seal the pocket by taking the heights of Mt. Ormel. In the morning of August 20, when the fog lifted, the Poles on Mt. Ormel and Americans on the St. Leonard ridge discovered the Dives river plain crawling with columns of Germans. Allied artillery took a murderous toll, but even so an estimated 20,000 to 40,000 men got out. However, most of the heavy equipment, tanks and artillery, was lost. In the pocket itself the carnage wrought during the final days was among the greatest yet seen in the war. An estimated 10,000 German dead were recorded, in some places hundreds lying almost shoulder to shoulder. The German horse-drawn transport left close to 2,000 horses scattered across the battlefield in pitiful piles, and another 3,000 were captured. The 90th U.S. Infantry Division alone, in four days fighting, claimed 13,000 prisoners, 8,000 Germans killed or wounded, 220 tanks, 130 half-tracks, 5,000 other vehicles, 990 guns and 2,000 trucks destroyed or captured. The U.S. losses were: 600 men killed; two anti-tank guns, six vehicles and five tanks destroyed. Between Argentan and Trun the British accounted for 187 tanks and self-propelled guns, 157 light light armored cars, 1,778 trucks, 669 cars, and 3,297 transport

Falaise Pocket

of all kinds. The harsh German losses in the Falaise pocket negated any thought of making a new stand behind the Seine river. The 5th Panzer Army and 7th Army were so weak and dispersed that they could do little more than continue their retreat. By late August the Allies would hold six major bridgeheads across the Seine.

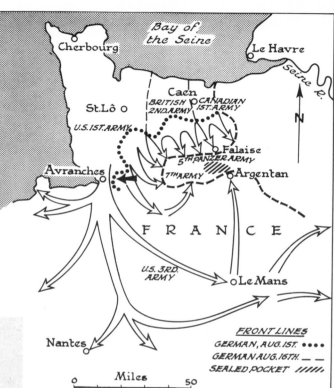

The Allied pincer action which sealed the Falaise Pocket.

A German Tiger II (B) destroyed in the Falaise gap. (IWM) Below right, a Panther that succumbed to the same fate

The Bold Lunge North

With the decisive destruction of the German armies in Normandy, the gates lay wide open to northern France. By the end of August British armor was across the Seine and the longest sustained advance for them in Europe had begun. The Canadian 1st and British 2nd Armies were hard pressed to keep up with the retreating Germans. Scout cars roared ahead of the main units, through village after village with little or no resistance. The advance continued night and day and soon it was realized that the main resistance would be crowds of well-wishers that flowed into the streets to greet them. The "Great Swan," as the advance became known, swept all the way to Brussels and Antwerp before the supply problems began to make themselves felt. Even so, Montgomery was convinced that the Allies should keep the pressure on and plunge into Holland. By September 8 they were across the Albert Canal and on the Dutch border. On September 17 the combined airborne and land attack at Arnhem went into action but fell on stiff German resistance and proved only partially successful.

Shermans of Canadian 1st Army.

British Crocodiles move north. These were flame-throwing Churchills which towed their fuel supply *(IWM)*

Americans Pierce the Siegfried Line

An American M-10 tank destroyer
moves through French street
on its way to the German border

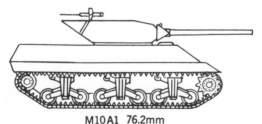

M10A1 76.2mm

With the liberation of Paris behind them, the American forces swept northeast through France. By mid-September Germany's Siegfried Line was in sight. Their progress had been uninterrupted with only the standard German rear-guard actions slowing the pace of advance. It was a totally motorized advance with everybody riding on tanks, tank destroyers, trucks, or jeeps. Fuel was the main concern, for Patton had stretched logistic lines to the utmost in his sweep to the German frontier. Hitler had ordered the ground in front of the Siegfreid Line to be held, but after three weeks of bloody fighting, Hodge's First Army pierced the line and took its first major German city, Aachen. In November some of the fiercest fighting of the war took place in the Hürtgen forest area, and Patton's armor made it across the Moselle river to take Metz. Now the Allies were obliged to take a breather in order to ensure adequate supply routes for their challenge on the Rhine.

G.I.'s and civilians examine a
Tiger I in the French town of Marle

Germans Ardennes Offensive

From a German army on the verge of collapse after defeats in France and Belgium, Hitler achieved the near impossible. He rebuilt a new army group on the Western Front that was not simply meant to hold ground, but was intended to strike a crushing blow against the weak Allied center. His plan was to sweep across Belgium and regain the port of Antwerp, thereby isolating the Allied northern armies. Once again he chose the heavily wooded Ardennes as his breakthrough point. He poured new blood into his 6th SS Panzer Army under Dietrich, and into the Panzer Lehr Division, in the form of new equipment including his reserves of Tiger 11's and Jagdtigers. However, much of the manpower was made up of ill-trained Volksgrenadier troops. The Fifth Panzer Army under General Manteuffel, and the 7th Army under Brandenberger were likewise stiffened up, while Field Marshal Model was given command of the operation. All their heavy equipment was quietly massed opposite the attack point. Twenty divisions, including seven armored, faced a front held by a mere six U.S. divisions of which one was armored. Just before dawn on December 15 German artillery pounded the U.S. lines, followed immediately by shock troops. Startled American

A German Tiger II rolls forward past a row of captured American prisoners.

troops held in many places, but panic forced many units to pull back in the face of overwhelming odds. However, for the Germans, the crucial road junctions of St. Vith and Bastogne proved to be stumbling blocks. Although St. Vith was overpowered after six days of bitter fighting, it threw off the German timetable seriously. Overcast conditions ruled out

American M-36 with 90mm gun, in winter camouflage

Allied air support. The Germans managed to skirt local resistance and had pushed sixty-five miles through American lines to within three miles of the Meuse river east of Dinant. At their zenith they suddenly suffered fuel shortages and at the same time met stiff Allied resistance on their extended fronts. By December 22 the weather had cleared and the full might of Allied air power was unleashed on the already staggering armored spearheads. On December 25 the U.S. 2nd Armored Division went over to the offensive and turned back the 2nd Panzer Division in its last attempt to reach the Meuse. The following day the U.S. 4th Armored broke through to relieve Bastogne. lowing day the U.S. 4th Armored broke through to relieve Bastogne.

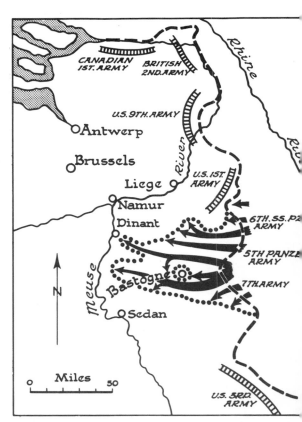

"The Bulge," Germany's final attempt to take the offensive in the west.

The Bulge Collapses

In the first few days of January the concerted Allied counterattack finally got under way. The German generals realized quite fully that any further attempt to renew their break for Antwerp was futile, but Hitler was determined to tie down Allied forces in the Bulge area by defending the ground taken. A weak attempt was made to stop Patton's northern drive on Houffalize. By this time Hodge's First Army was applying pressure from the north. During this first week of January the weather remained overcast with raw winds and snow flurries. Clearing the Germans from the contested areas under those conditions proved to be a slow job. This campaign was costly to both

M4A4 "Sherman" 75mm

Above, left, a Sherman being replenished with 75mm shells. Above, M4A1 Sherman with 76mm gun and sandbag reinforcement

sides: the Americans suffered losses amounting to 81,000 killed, wounded or captured; the British 1,400 casualties. The Germans lost close to 100,000 killed, wounded or captured. Approximately 800 tanks were lost to each side; however, the Allied losses

were far more easily replaced than those of the Germans. By January 22 the weather cleared and Allied planes once more nullified any further supply attempts by the Germans. The last vestige of the Bulge had disappeared by the end of the month.

Russians Reach Out for Berlin

By January 26 the Russian 5th Guards Tank Army was in full control of the Baltic coast northeast of Elbing, and the German 4th Army and 3rd Panzer Army in East Prussia were cut off. Within the first week of February the Russians were on the Oder River only 35 miles from Berlin. The 2nd Belorussian Front moved forward on February 10 but they met dogged resistance and the advance was slow. The Russian Front was stretched well beyond its supply and air support bases, and several German counterattacks put severe pressure on the forward lines. By mid-February Marshal Zhukov was on the Oder at Frankfurt and Kuestrin. Koniev was on the Neisse sixty miles beyond Breslau, with less than one hundred miles to reach Prague. The Red Army had covered 275 miles in three weeks, clearing most of Poland and overrunning the coal fields and industries of Silesia. On the Danube Front, encircled Budapest fell on February 13 after seven weeks of savage house-to-house fighting, and within two months Vienna would also be taken.

A Russian T-34/85 column moving through a ravaged East Prussian town

Crossing the Rhine

The Germans had chosen to stand west of the Rhine by flooding vast areas of lowland and making Allied progress in the north very difficult. With the crossing at Remagen by the U.S. 9th Armored on March 7 the Germans were forced to drain off reserves from the northern defenses. By March 23 the British 2nd and Canadian 1st Army units were across the Rhine west of Wesel. The combined Allied forces swept the Rhine area clear of German resistance and encircled a huge force trapped in the Ruhr basin. Meanwhile the Canadian 5th Armored Division was given the chore of cleaning up German troops still isolated in Holland and the coastal areas.

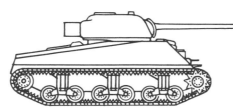

M4 Sherman VC "Fire Fly" 76.2mm

Left, a Canadian Badger flamethrower converted from the Canadian-built Ram tank. Above, Sherman 17 pounder of 5th Canadian Armored Div. moving through Putten, Holland. The camouflage on the gun was intended to make the heavier gun indistinguishable from 75mm models. Note various track types on side and front, used for additional protection, and grousers on tracks

German Resistance Collapses

By April 18 the Allied forces had cut the Ruhr pocket to shreds, and with the Saar and Silesia already overrun, all of Germany's major industrial regions were under Allied control. Since the Ruhr battle had exhausted the last of her forces, Germany was now left with little to defend Berlin from the west. Throughout April the German defenses had crumbled ev-

Right, flail tank of 5th Canadian Armored moving through Putten, Holland
Above, Sherman VC Firefly bearing the deadly 17 pounder gun carrying troops of the Canadian Royal H.L.I. Note appliqué camouflage.

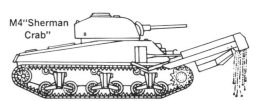

M4"Sherman Crab"

Hostilities End in Europe

erywhere and now Zhukov and Koniev struck at Berlin with their huge tank armies. After twelve days of savage struggle the capital of the Third Reich fell on May 2. Patton's Third Army had rolled across the Czech border on May 5 and could have captured all of Bohemia and liberated Prague. However, a previous agreement with the Russians

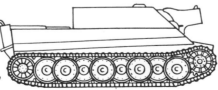

StuPzVI"SturmTiger"

Left, an abandoned German Sturmtiger built to launch the 36cm rocket mortar. Above, a German StuG. III and Hetzer remain as part of the rubble in central Prague, May 9, 1945 *(Kliment)*

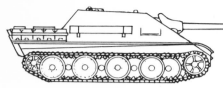

"JagdPanther" 88mm

precluded this move and the liberation of Czechoslovakia was handed
over to the Red Army. Meanwhile,
Eisenhower assigned units from the
U.S. Ninth Army to Montgomery to
help seal off the Germans in Denmark and beat the Russians to the
Baltic. By May 8 the final surrender
had been signed and the war in Europe came to a close.

A Canadian officer surveys
captured German equipment
from atop a Jagdpanther

A Cross Section of WW2 Tank Ammunition

These drawings show the comparative size of some of the armor-piercing and high-explosive ammunition used by the various armies during the war. The drawings have been reduced here to the scale of one-inch equals one-foot.

1 US 37mm AP (M-3 Stuart)
2 German 37mm AP (PzKpfw. III)
3 British 2-pounder AP (Crusader I-II, Matilda, Tetrarch)
4 Italian 47mm
5 German 47mm AP, HE (PzJager I)
6 German 50mm (Short) AP (PzKpfw. III)
7 German 50mm KwK.39 (Long) HE (PzKpfw. III)
8 British 6-pounder AP (Crusader III, Cromwell I-III, Valentine VIII-IX, Churchill III-IV)
9 Russian 57mm AP (SU-57)
10 German 75mm (Short) HE (PzKpfw. III-IV)
11 British 6-pounder APDS (Cromwell I-III, Valentine VIII-IX)
12 German 75mm KwK. 40 (Long) HE (PzKpfw. IV)
13 Russian 76.2mm HE (T-34/76, KV-1, SU-76)
14 German 128mm PAK.44 AP (Jagdtiger)
15 German 88mm KwK.43 HE (Tiger II)
16 US 90mm HE (M-36, M-26)
17 German 88mm KwK.36 HE (Tiger I)
18 Russian 85mm AP (T-34/85, KV-85, SU-85)
19 German 75mm KwK.42 AP (Panther)
20 British 17-pounder APDS (Sherman VC Firefly)
21 US 75mm HE (M-3 Grant, M-4 Sherman)
22 British 77mm AP (Comet)

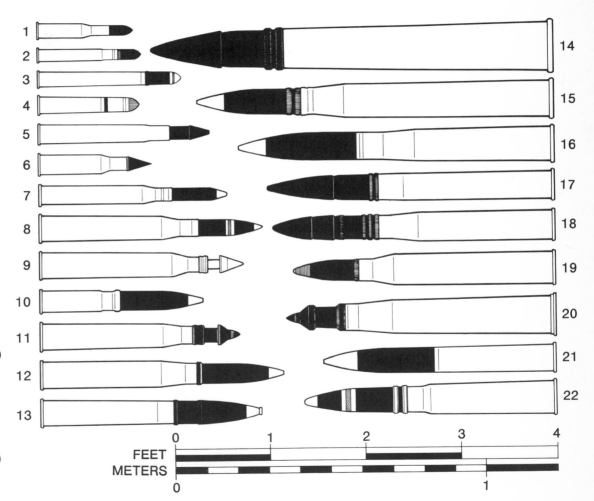

FEET
METERS

MORE BOOKS ABOUT TANKS YOU'LL WANT TO OWN

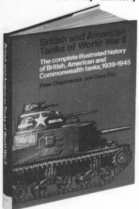